W9-BBV-062

Daniel Webster

Other titles in *Historical American Biographies*

DANIEL WEBSTER

"Liberty *and* Union, Now and Forever"

Bonnie Carman Harvey

Enslow Publishers, Inc.

40 Industrial Road	PO Box 38
Box 398	Aldershot
Berkeley Heights, NJ 07922	Hants GU12 6BP
USA	UK

http://www.enslow.com

Library of Congress Cataloging-in-Publication Data

Harvey, Bonnie C.

Daniel Webster : liberty and union, now and forever / Bonnie Carman Harvey.
     p. cm. — (Historical American biographies)
Includes bibliographical references and index.
ISBN 0-7660-1392-8
1. Webster, Daniel, 1782–1852—Juvenile literature. 2. Webster, Daniel,
1782–1852—Oratory—Juvenile literature. 3. United States—Politics and
government—1815–1861—Juvenile literature. 4. Legislators—United States—
Biography—Juvenile literature. 5. United States. Congress. Senate—Biography—
Juvenile literature. 6. Political oratory—United States—History—19th century—
Juvenile literature. I. Title. II. Series.
     E340.W4 H28   2001
     973.5'092—dc21   00-009662

Printed in the United States of America

10 9 8 7 6 5 4 3 2 1

To Our Readers: We have done our best to make sure all Internet addresses in this book
were active and appropriate when we went to press. However, the author and the pub-
lisher have no control over and assume no liability for the material available on those
Internet sites or on other Web sites they may link to. Any comments or suggestions can be
sent by e-mail to comments@enslow.com or to the address on the back cover.

CONTENTS

Famous American artist Chester Harding painted this portrait of Daniel Webster in 1845.

1

THE HAYNE DEBATE

L iberty *and* Union, now and forever, one and inseparable!"[1] Daniel Webster's final statement in his debate with Senator Robert Y. Hayne of South Carolina resounded through the Senate chamber on January 26, 1830.

Webster's reply to Hayne actually took place during a second debate between the two men. Senator Thomas Hart Benton of Missouri had prompted the debate when he opposed a suggestion to limit Western land sales. By limiting land sales, the Northern states would be able to stop the westward movement of the country. They could also stop the Western and Southern states that had banded together to promote their mutual interests—cheap land and low tariffs (taxes paid on imported or exported goods).

For the previous six years, Senator Benton had pressed for a freer distribution of public lands. He hoped to build up the West at the expense of the East, so that more Western states could come into the Union as slaveholding states. Daniel Webster opposed the Benton plan. He was greatly concerned about what it represented.

After Senator Benton's opening argument, Robert Hayne, a suave South Carolina senator, stepped in. He offered sympathy and support to the West on behalf of his native South. He also suggested that the West and South should unite in self-defense against the North.

At first, Southerners were divided on the plan, but they eventually made up their minds to support Western land claims in exchange for Western support of their free trade policy. President Andrew Jackson, in fact, had won the presidency because of the support of this West-South combination.

Thus, when Senator Samuel A. Foote proposed in early January 1830 to withdraw public lands from sale, Senator Benton was quick to claim that the resolution showed New England's selfishness. Soon, Southerners rallied to Benton's side and the debate began.

Daniel Webster had enjoyed a brief rest from his government duties during December 1829. He had also taken a short honeymoon with his new wife. Now, Webster relished the opportunity to get back to work.

On January 19, 1830, following Benton's opening Senate argument the previous day, Robert Hayne

Robert Hayne (seen here) was Daniel Webster's adversary in the debate that made both men famous.

picked up the debate. While Hayne was speaking, Webster stopped by the Senate. Webster later wrote about the suddenness of his being drawn into the debate: "The whole matter was quite unexpected. . . . I went into the Senate, and Mr. Hayne . . . just then arose. When he sat down, my friends said he must be answered, and I thought so too."[2] Webster courageously took the floor the next day.

Webster jumped into the battle with glee on the morning of January 20. He decided to turn the issue from the sale of Western lands to the more basic ones of constitutional law, states' rights, and nullification (when a state refuses to recognize a federal law). He knew that these were the important issues.

Webster addressed the matter of Western land sales in his initial speech. He emphasized that, if too much acreage were suddenly put up for sale at cheap prices, land speculators would buy it. They would end up competing with the federal government for profit. He also stated that finding enough settlers for all this land in the West would be next to impossible.

Webster then turned his address to the Union itself. He stressed the common bond that all the states shared in regard to Western lands. He spoke at length about the word *consolidation*—particularly as it related to the Union. Webster pointed out the importance of the states' looking toward the interests they had in common instead of focusing on issues that would separate or divide them. Webster was trying to say that the Union should be supreme, both in terms of power and in the loyalty of the American people.

Hayne's reply focused on a state's right to nullify, or void, federal legislation. Hayne said it was wrong for the federal government to act by itself in certain decisions. The states, too, should be considered. Hayne heartily endorsed states' rights. He declared, "The very life of our system is the independence of the States and . . . there is no evil more to be deprecated [disapproved] than the consolidation of this Government."[3]

Webster was concerned after hearing Hayne's words. He sensed that the emphasis on individual states' rights, as opposed to the power of the federal government, would limit the future growth, prosperity, and greatness of the nation.

Webster was much better prepared for the second debate, which began on January 25, 1830. He did not begin to speak, however, until Tuesday, January 26. Much excitement surrounded Webster's Senate speech. The chamber began to fill with people around 9:00 A.M.

As Webster got up to make his speech, he had an air of confidence. His voice was clear, calm, and strong. First, he asked that the resolution on Western land sales that was being considered by the Senate be read. Webster then proceeded to shred Hayne's argument.

In his speech, Webster mentioned his position on slavery. He stated, "The slavery of the South has always been regarded as a matter of domestic policy, left with the States themselves, and with which the federal government had nothing to do. Certainly, Sir, I am, and ever have been, of that opinion."[4] Webster assured the South that he did not intend to outlaw slavery. He was concerned mainly with keeping the United States together in a time of growing division.

An artist depicted Daniel Webster's powerful presence (center) as he made his famous reply to Senator Hayne.

Webster then turned his attention to the Union itself, stressing the bond that united the individual states. He cited the Constitution, to try to show its intent with regard to the states versus the federal government. His appeal rang through the Senate Chamber: "I go for the Constitution as it is, and for the Union as it is. . . . It is, Sir, the people's Constitution, the people's government, made for the people, made by the people, and answerable to the people."[5]

Webster not only made a great showing in the debate with Hayne that day, but he won a tremendous victory as a defender of the Constitution. Webster's speech and ideas in the debate would later help educate the nation about the strength of the Constitution of the United States.

Webster's speech was a rallying call to the country. People began to feel they were part of a nation, instead of just their own state. A growing patriotism developed, and with it, Daniel Webster's name became a household term.

2

BOYHOOD DAYS

Daniel Webster's background held little promise of the fame he would later enjoy. His family on both sides boasted of tough ancestors who knew how to battle bears, wolves, American Indians, and the rocky New Hampshire soil. For one hundred fifty years, they had survived against difficult odds in the harsh New England climate. Before Daniel was born, four generations of Websters had lived in New England.

In 1636, sixteen years after the Pilgrims landed at Plymouth, Massachusetts, Thomas Webster came to America with his mother, Margaret Webster Godfrey. Together, they moved to the coast at Hampton, New Hampshire.

After Thomas married, his wife had five sons, one of whom was named Ebenezer. In 1667, Thomas and his family lived in the farming community of Kingston, New Hampshire. His son Ebenezer, who married Hannah Judkins, would become the father of nine sons, the eldest of whom was also named Ebenezer.

This younger Ebenezer Webster married Susannah Bachelder, who was a descendant of the Reverend Stephen Bachelder, the first settled clergyman in New Hampshire. Susannah was brave, determined, and full of energy. Their eldest son, another Ebenezer, was born on April 22, 1739, in Kingston. He would one day become Daniel Webster's father.

While he was still a boy, Ebenezer enlisted with a soldiers' group called Roger's Rangers, which fought in the French and Indian War. He was involved in an invasion of Canada, serving under Sir Jeffrey Amherst. Following the war, in 1763, as a reward for his service, twenty-four-year-old Ebenezer received a large grant of land from Benning Wentworth, the royal governor of New Hampshire. He decided to call his new town Stevenstown. Sometime later, the name changed to Salisbury. Located near the center of New Hampshire, the township benefited from the nearby convergence of two streams that formed the Merrimack River.

Ebenezer Webster's Rugged Life

Ebenezer Webster chose to live on a section of 225 acres at the town's northernmost end. He and his family faced many hardships in the isolated New Hampshire wilderness: savage winters with enormous

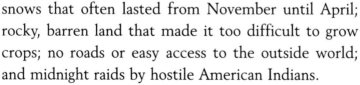

French and Indian War

The first battle of the French and Indian War took place in 1755. The war was fought between the French and the British for control of America. General Edward Braddock was in charge of the British and colonial troops, a somewhat disorganized fighting force. After several defeats, King George II of England put Secretary of State William Pitt in charge of the war effort. Pitt selected outstanding generals to lead the British troops in battle. The French Fort Duquesne fell to the British in July 1758. The following summer, Fort Niagara, in New York, was taken. By 1760, Montreal had fallen to the British Army. With this defeat, the French abandoned Canada to the English. The 1763 Treaty of Paris ended the fighting and gave Canada and the eastern half of the Mississippi Valley to the British. France was allowed to keep only two small islands in the St. Lawrence River.

snows that often lasted from November until April; rocky, barren land that made it too difficult to grow crops; no roads or easy access to the outside world; and midnight raids by hostile American Indians.

Full of courage and endurance, Ebenezer also showed uncommon strength of character. Daniel Webster would revere his father. Remembering Ebenezer in later years, Daniel said he saw in him "what I collect to have been the character of some of the old Puritans. He was deeply religious . . . yet having a heart in him that he seemed to have borrowed from a lion."[1]

Ebenezer married Mehitable Smith. Together, they had five children, three of whom lived to maturity: Susannah, David, and Joseph. When Mehitable died in March 1774, Ebenezer looked for another wife quickly. His oldest child, Susannah, was just eight years old. A man remarried as soon as possible on the frontier. He needed help raising his children and performing household chores. Acting on the suggestion of his brother's wife, Ebenezer called on Abigail "Nabby" Eastman, a seamstress who was visiting relatives in Salisbury. Five months later, in August 1774, the two were married.

The American Revolution gave Ebenezer Webster another chance to fight in the military. This time, he joined with his fellow colonists to free the American colonies from British rule. Although he commanded troops from New Hampshire in several battles, Ebenezer still found time for his family.

Family Life

At thirty-seven, Abigail Webster had been a spinster until she married Ebenezer. Although she was rather heavyset and plain, Abigail was tender and understanding. She was also highly intelligent. Her ancestors had come to America from Wales in 1636. Like her husband, Abigail had a rugged pioneer spirit.

Abigail and Ebenezer Webster had five children over the next ten years. The first two were girls:

Mehitable, born in 1775, and Abigail, born in 1778. The first son, Ezekiel, or "Zeke," was born on March 11, 1778. Daniel arrived on January 18, 1782, in the same year as Martin Van Buren, John C. Calhoun, and Thomas Hart Benton—three men who would play major roles in his later life.

Just before Daniel was born, dramatic events were taking place in the course of the American Revolution that would dramatically affect him later. In 1781, American General George Washington defeated British troops under the command of British General Charles Cornwallis at Yorktown, Virginia. Although a peace treaty would not be signed until 1783, the revolution was, for the most part, over. The former British colonies were now the independent United States of America.

Early Impressions

The Webster family had moved to a frame house a few years before Daniel was born, but he always boasted that his brothers and sisters (except for younger sister, Sarah) had had the privilege of being born in a log cabin. In January 1784, the family moved again, this time to the small township of Salisbury Lower Village, where Ebenezer had bought a fairly large house.

Daniel Webster later remembered growing up in the picturesque valley where the house had been built. Once, when he was eight, a constant two-day rain saturated the house and the grounds. So much rain fell, in fact, that the river overflowed its banks. The Websters watched as a huge, hay-filled barn belonging

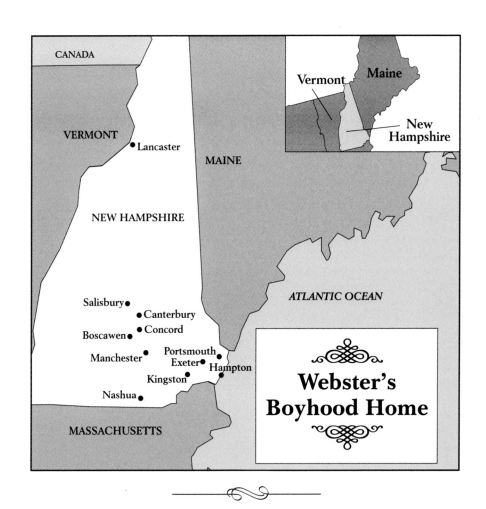

CANADA

VERMONT
● Lancaster

MAINE

NEW HAMPSHIRE

Salisbury ●
● Canterbury
Boscawen ● ● Concord
Manchester ● Portsmouth ●
Exeter ● Hampton
Kingston ●
Nashua ●

MASSACHUSETTS

ATLANTIC OCEAN

Vermont Maine

New
Hampshire

Webster's
Boyhood Home

This map shows the areas in New Hampshire where Daniel Webster was born and spent his childhood.

to a neighbor floated down the river. At that point, the family thought about fleeing to some nearby mountains. Luckily, the rain soon ceased and the flood waters went down.[2]

Daniel realized at an early age that he was different from the other children in his town. Daniel's father helped set him apart from other children because Ebenezer Webster was the best-known and most respected man in the community. He was also by far the biggest in physical build.

Daniel himself, although of slight build, was somewhat peculiar-looking. He had an unusually large head that was crowned with bushy, jet-black hair, and he had huge black eyes. Because of his appearance, the local men began to call Daniel "little Black Dan" before his tenth birthday.[3]

Daniel's desire to read and his enjoyment of school also showed that he was different from other children. It seemed he had always been able to read. Daniel had an amazing memory and remembered everything that he read.

Early School Days

Daniel's first school days took place in a log cabin. But the local schools, which taught only reading and writing, did not stay in one location. They shifted from one place in town to another so that all the school-age children could benefit. Because of the unstable nature of the schools, Daniel realized early on that he would have to educate himself by reading books. Although books were scarce, Daniel read every one he could find. He discovered books by the English writers Joseph Addison and Alexander Pope. He also mastered Latin grammar.

Although Daniel, who never liked farm work, could not contribute much to his father's farm, he did work at his father's sawmill. He would set the saw, then read while the boards were being cut. Others in the family made fun of his lack of ability in the rough-hewn farm life, but Daniel did not mind. He would rather read than work in the fields any day.

Daniel was closest to his brother Ezekiel. "Zeke" was four years older and had a robust build like his father's. Even though Daniel admired Zeke, especially for physical ability, Daniel claimed that he was smarter. One night, he and Zeke got into an argument over the exact wording of a poem they had read in an almanac. Daniel refused to let the matter rest. He lit a candle and went to another room to find the poem and check its wording. When he found out he was

Joseph Addison

An English essayist and poet, Addison's witty and elegant works appeared in magazines such as *The Tatler*, founded by Richard Steele in 1709, and *The Spectator*, founded by Addison and Steele together in 1711. Addison often addressed the issue of good manners. He urged women to take the lead in their families and be a good influence on their husbands and children.

wrong, he went back to bed. Unfortunately, he failed to put out the candle properly and nearly burned down the house!

Thomas Thompson, a newcomer to the town, was a Harvard graduate and lawyer. He became a staunch supporter of the young Webster. Thirteen-year-old Daniel worked in Thompson's office for a time as a receptionist. Daniel impressed Thompson with his intelligence and curiosity. The lawyer told Ebenezer to send Daniel away to a good school. None of the Webster children had gone away to school. In fact, only two residents in all of Salisbury had ever gone to college. Ebenezer, who often struggled to manage his farm and money, had to think long and hard about the lawyer's suggestion.

After realizing that Daniel, the brightest of the Webster children, was not cut out for farm work, Ebenezer made a decision. Daniel recalled their conversation years later. He and his father were working in the hayfield together when the Honorable Abiel Foster from Canterbury came to visit. Daniel did not consider Foster a particularly outstanding individual, even though he knew Foster was college-educated. After Foster left, Daniel's father called Daniel over and told him that Foster was a worthy man, a member of Congress, and that he earned six dollars a day while Ebenezer toiled in the field doing hard physical labor for much less money. The reason, according to Daniel's father, was that Foster had an education. Ebenezer noted that he had missed his own chance to get an education, so now he had to do farm work. He told Daniel:

> My child . . . I could not give your elder brothers the advantages of knowledge, but I can do something for you. Exert yourself, improve your opportunities, learn, learn, and when I am gone, you will not need to go through the hardships which I have undergone, and which have made me an old man before my time.[4]

Phillips Academy

On May 25, 1796, Daniel and his father rode to Exeter, New Hampshire, on horseback to enroll Daniel in the Phillips Academy. To fourteen-year-old Webster, who had never been away from home before, the school seemed huge.

Benjamin Abbot, a well-known schoolmaster of the era, presided over the school. Daniel easily passed the entrance exam, which required little more than being able to read the Bible. Still, he continued to feel ill at ease for a time among the ninety boys attending the academy. They had expensive clothes and confident manners. They seemed able to translate easily from the classics and could do mathematical calculations quickly. With his homemade clothes, clumsy boots, and rough table manners, young Daniel felt out of place. Nevertheless, he tried to do his best at school.

For someone who would later become an outstanding orator, at this time in his life, Daniel often became paralyzed with fear when he tried to give a speech, or declamation. Every attempt he made at

Phillips Academy ended in failure. He would return to his room and burst into tears over his embarrassment.

The Schoolteacher

By December 1796, Ebenezer thought his son Daniel, now nearly fifteen, was ready to become a teacher in the local school. Ebenezer took Daniel out of the Phillips Academy and put him to work in a one-room school in Salisbury.

A few weeks later, Dr. Samuel Wood from nearby Boscawen remarked to Ebenezer that his son could do more than teach at a poor quality local school. Wood offered to prepare Daniel for Dartmouth College. Ebenezer agreed. In February 1797, he packed Daniel into a sleigh and started toward Boscawen.

On to Dartmouth

Ebenezer's decision to provide further schooling for his son would change Daniel's life. At the time, only about two out of every one thousand Americans went to college. Those who did receive such an advanced education were virtually assured of becoming part of an elite group of merchants, property owners, and professionals that made up the upper class of American society. They were also the nation's political leaders.

Dr. Samuel Wood recognized Daniel's special abilities and offered to tutor him and help with his living expenses. A Dartmouth graduate himself, Wood was a minister in one of the churches in the Merrimack Valley.

From February to August 1797, Daniel Webster studied Greek and the Latin classics. He also enjoyed the Boscawen Social Library, where he read works by John Milton, Alexander Pope, Francis Thompson, and William Cowper.

In August, he returned to Salisbury and prepared to make the trip to Dartmouth. The Dartmouth student body consisted of one hundred forty male students. It was one of the largest colleges in the nation. Most Dartmouth students were at least four years older than fifteen-year-old Daniel Webster. Despite his youth and his somewhat limited college preparation, Webster applied himself to his studies vigorously. His ability to focus all his intellectual energy on a single point and his excellent memory allowed him to do well in class. One of Daniel's classmates remembered that Webster could read a twenty-page passage two times and repeat it almost word for word.[5]

College Leadership

Before long, freshman Daniel Webster had joined the United Fraternity, one of the leading literary societies on campus. The group soon began meeting in his room. With the practice he had as a member of the group, by his junior year, Webster was receiving acclaim for his speeches. Daniel had at last overcome his fear of public speaking, which would be important to his future career.

Although he was not an outstanding student, Webster did well enough to be elected to Phi Beta

Kappa, an honorary academic organization, in his junior year. He became known for writing poetry, too. Although much of what he wrote was not very memorable, his poetry reading made him a huge success all over campus as he dramatically acted out each poem.

Webster's college career began to point to an interest in politics. He was learning to use language to gain favor and social advancement. The Fourth of July speech he gave during his junior year might be viewed as his first political triumph. It showed Webster's considerable maturity despite his youth.

Webster started his speech by discussing the heroic events that led up to the American Revolution and the creation of a new nation. He called the United States Constitution "undoubtedly the greatest approximation toward human perfection the political world ever yet experienced . . . which, perhaps, will forever stand in the history of mankind, without a parallel."[6]

Just as Webster changed from a shy boy to a powerful speaker, his personal style also changed considerably during his college years. No longer did he wear homespun clothing. He ran up large bills at a local general store for cotton stockings, silk gloves, and velvet trousers. His purchases included gin, brandy, port wine, lemons, and sugar. Webster went into debt. He was not concerned, however. His father had always been in debt, yet had remained well-respected in the community.

As his senior year at college came to a close, Webster was not chosen by the faculty to give either of the two addresses at the college's graduation ceremonies. This caused the young man, who had great ambition for a bright future, terrible distress. This oversight on the part of the Dartmouth faculty would mark one of the last times in his life that Daniel Webster would not give the main speech at any public function he attended.

3

Young Man
on the Move

When he returned to Salisbury as a college
graduate in the fall of 1801, Daniel Webster
struggled against boredom. At Dartmouth, he had
enjoyed the free exchange of ideas, books by great
authors, and other intellectual stimulation. Salisbury
now seemed dull to him. Although he planned to con-
tinue his studies in the law office of Thomas
Thompson, he knew that even this would seem bleak
compared to his college days.

Although Webster had not actually chosen law as
his profession, he preferred it to the two other pro-
fessions available to well-educated young men like
him—theology and medicine. But studying law books
as opposed to literary classics seemed uninspiring. In
addition, Webster disliked helping Thompson with

petty cases involving the local farmers. Such simple issues failed to challenge him.

Change of Direction

By January 1802, Webster's father needed financial help with farm expenses and to pay tuition for Daniel's brother Ezekiel, who was now attending college. So Webster left Salisbury for Fryeburg, Maine, to become an academy schoolmaster.

He roomed with a Dartmouth friend named Jacob McGaw. The two boarded with the local register of deeds and had access to the library of Judah Dana, a Fryeburg attorney. Webster's time there turned out to be much like his days at Dartmouth. He enjoyed reading history and literature, copying deeds (to pay for his board), and having discussions with McGaw. He wrote to a Salisbury friend: "Nothing here is unpleasant. . . . The people treat me with kindness, and I have the fortune to find myself in a very good family. I see little female company. . . ."[1]

The good performance of his students at Fryeburg Academy showed Webster's ability as a schoolmaster. The trustees of the school awarded him a special monetary gift and the honor of giving a Fourth of July oration. But Webster knew he did not want to spend the rest of his life teaching school. He felt it would not be challenging enough. So he decided to return to Salisbury and resume his law studies with Thomas Thompson in the fall of 1802. Webster continued to struggle, however, with the idea of making the law his profession.

Journey to Boston

Back in Salisbury, Webster soon began to get restless again. He sensed that he needed to be in a larger city with more opportunities. When his brother Ezekiel, who had graduated from Dartmouth and was now teaching at Short Street School in Boston, invited Daniel to come to Boston and tutor some of his pupils in Greek and Latin in exchange for room and board, Webster jumped at the chance. He arrived in Boston on July 17, 1804.

As a stranger in the city, it was difficult for Webster to make connections with a good lawyer with whom he could study. Eventually, he persuaded Christopher Gore to tutor him. Gore had been one of New England's leading politicians ever since President George Washington had named him the first United States district attorney for Massachusetts in 1789. That Webster was able to convince a well-known lawyer like Gore to tutor him demonstrates just how persuasive the young man was.[2]

Webster came to respect Gore a great deal. Gore was not only an outstanding attorney but also a scholar with many interests. Webster loved Gore's library. It held volumes by writers such as Francis Bacon, a sixteenth-century English statesman and philosopher; and Charles Viner, a seventeenth-century English lawyer. The Boston courts provided Webster with the opportunity to observe the practice of law at its finest. Webster began to see the legal profession as a new challenge and to find his studies less boring.

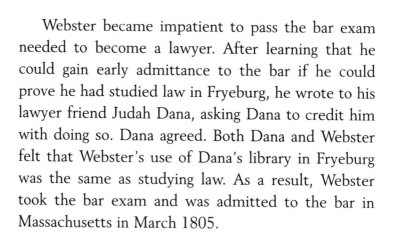

Charles Viner

A legal scholar who was born in Salisbury, Wiltshire, England, Viner studied law at Oxford University. He never qualified for the bar and never actually practiced. However, he compiled a massive *Abridgement of the Law of England* in twenty-three volumes between 1741 and 1756. When he died, he left most of his estate to Oxford University. With the inheritance, Oxford was able to found the Vinerian Scholarships to help worthy students who needed financial aid.

Webster became impatient to pass the bar exam needed to become a lawyer. After learning that he could gain early admittance to the bar if he could prove he had studied law in Fryeburg, he wrote to his lawyer friend Judah Dana, asking Dana to credit him with doing so. Dana agreed. Both Dana and Webster felt that Webster's use of Dana's library in Fryeburg was the same as studying law. As a result, Webster took the bar exam and was admitted to the bar in Massachusetts in March 1805.

First Days as an Attorney

Eager to get started with his practice, Webster opened a law office in Boscawen, New Hampshire, to be near his sixty-six-year-old father, who suffered bouts of ill health. Although Webster's practice flourished in Boscawen, he had to content himself with handling small-town legal matters such as uncollected debts.

Only occasionally did Webster actually get a chance to try a case before a jury.

His father died in April 1806. Soon after, Webster moved to Portsmouth, New Hampshire, leaving his brother Ezekiel, now a lawyer himself, to take over the Boscawen practice. Just before he left for Portsmouth, Webster wrote to the Reverend Thomas Worcester, minister of the Congregational Church of Salisbury, expressing his religious beliefs and his desire to unite with the church. A short time later, Webster joined the church. This was an important step in society for a promising young lawyer.

Marriage

Marriage was all that remained for Webster to complete his preparation for a successful career. Webster accomplished this final step after courting Grace Fletcher, a minister's daughter from Salisbury. Webster had known Grace for a few years, but now he was ready to propose. A fairly well-educated woman for her day, Grace had taught school and shared Webster's small-town upbringing. The two were married in the spring of 1808. With his lovely wife behind him, Webster finally felt ready for the challenges that lay ahead.

The Websters bought a house in a fashionable neighborhood in Portsmouth. Webster set up his law office near Market Square—a reputable address. Portsmouth, a thriving seaport, was an exciting place to live.

Grace Fletcher Webster as she looked in 1827, when Chester Harding painted this portrait.

Grace and Daniel Webster made a graceful couple. They carried on an active social life in their new hometown. They soon made many friends in the town's upper social circles.

Sometime after moving to Portsmouth, Webster's physical appearance began to change. His complexion grew darker, more like his father's had been, and his body began to fill out. Webster became so striking that some of his friends compared him to a lion with his commanding speech and presence.[3]

Before long, Webster found himself in close contact with many of New Hampshire's leading attorneys, both in courtrooms across the state and in the state's scattered inns and taverns. Lawyers of the time often had to travel great distances to argue their cases.

Influential Connections

Much of Webster's time in Portsmouth was spent following the Superior Court sessions throughout the counties of New Hampshire. Gradually, Webster refined and sharpened his oratorical skills. William Plumer, a well-known attorney, said of Webster: "As a speaker merely he is perhaps the best at the bar. His language is correct, his gestures good, and his delivery slow, articulate, and distinct. [And] he excels in the statement of facts. . . ."[4]

Webster's fame began to spread through his writing as well as his speaking. Some of the early articles he wrote appeared in the prestigious Boston-based magazine *Monthly Anthology*. The publication featured pieces by some of the leading intellectuals of New

England. For the most part, *Anthology* represented the views of New England Federalists; in fact, the magazine expressed a concern about their decline in power. The Federalist party, formed in the 1790s, was largely made up of well-off Northerners, including merchants, financiers, and factory owners. Some Southerners who owned large plantations were also Federalists. Most Federalists distrusted ordinary Americans. They preferred to have aristocratic men such as John Adams and Alexander Hamilton lead them. They also favored a strong central government and a national bank that would protect their property and businesses from foreign competition.

A true Federalist, Webster felt all the concerns expressed in the *Anthology*. When Webster gave the Phi Beta Kappa address at Dartmouth in the summer of 1809, his speech could have come directly from the pages of the magazine. He spoke against the "love of gold" in America and urged a pursuit of literary interests instead.[5]

Starting a Family

In April 1810, the Websters celebrated the birth of their first child, Grace. The little girl brought much joy to the Webster household.

Daniel Webster's ability both as a lawyer and as an orator was increasing rapidly. In time, his skill would enable him to make a sizeable fortune.

4

UP-AND-COMING
CONGRESSMAN

From the time he was a young boy, Webster had
been taught to revere the first United States president, George Washington, and his politics. New
Hampshire's politics, in particular, were based on
Federalist ideas and Washington's beliefs. The politicians of Webster's boyhood believed in democratic
self-government. However, they were in favor of having a core group of individuals speak for the rest of the
people. In small towns like Salisbury, where Webster
grew up, the local leaders made up that core. His
father, Ebenezer, had been one of these individuals.

Federalists and Republicans

Nevertheless, by the time Webster was established in
Portsmouth, the state's politics had changed a great

The members of the Federalist party greatly admired George Washington, whose political beliefs were similar to their own.

deal. A new Republican governor had replaced Federalist John Gilman in 1804. The Democratic-Republican party, which was led by President Thomas Jefferson, was made up of farmers, small planters, workers, and craftsmen who came mainly from rural areas and the frontier. These people looked to the Constitution and to state governments to protect them from the power of the federal government. They distrusted the well-to-do eastern aristocrats whom the Federalists wanted to have in charge of the government. New Hampshire had now come into the Republican fold. Webster worked hard to try to convince the town leaders to return to Federalist policies.

In December 1807, the United States Congress passed the Embargo Act. This law prevented the importation of foreign goods and the exportation of American goods. It was passed in response to the habit England and France, which were at war, had of interfering with American ships at sea. The English were known to take sailors off American ships and force them to work on British vessels. President Jefferson hoped the Embargo Act would put economic pressure on England and France, since they would be unable to buy American goods, and force them to leave American ships alone. However, the Embargo Act proved to be disastrous to trade for towns such as Portsmouth. The law caused many New Hampshire coastal merchants to lose money.

In the fall of 1808, Daniel Webster wrote a pamphlet attacking the Embargo Act. He believed the act would destroy American commerce. The Embargo Act was eventually repealed, although Webster's pamphlet probably had little impact on the decision.[1]

Entering Politics

By 1812, Webster was elected head of the Portsmouth town council. He became the town's first Federalist leader in thirteen years. In a Fourth of July address, Webster compared former President Washington's wise policy of neutrality toward England with new President James Madison's current policy. Madison was trying in vain to make the seas safe for American sailors. He had imposed a new embargo on England, causing many merchants to lose money once again. Madison's policies were extremely harmful to trade in the city of Portsmouth.

By August 1812, thirty-year-old Webster had become the voice of New Hampshire Federalists. When one of Portsmouth's leading citizens, Jeremiah Smith, asked him to run for a seat in the House of Representatives, Webster refused. He said he could

Gilbert Stuart painted this portrait of Webster as he looked around 1817.

not take the time away from his law office. The next day, however, Webster changed his mind. He noted: "As to the law, I must attend to that too—but honor after all is worth more than money."[2] He easily won the nomination and election.

As he left for Washington, D.C., in the spring of 1813, at the age of thirty-one, Daniel Webster seemed to have everything a person could want. His close friends and acquaintances spoke highly of his amazing powers of memory and speech. One of Webster's close friends, George T. Curtis, offered the following comments:

> I can scarcely open one of the numerous commun-
> ications that are before me from those who knew him
> as a young man, that does not speak with peculiar zeal
> of his general powers. It seems as if they felt that the
> world had set its seal upon all that was great in his
> genius and majestic in his deportment and character
> or imposing in his intellectual achievements and
> public service, yet that there was a charm, a grace, a
> perfume in his social existence which they fear the
> world has not known, and of which they bear their
> testimony more fondly than of all things else that
> cluster about his name.[3]

Although Webster had incredible talent, he had flaws as well. He could cut someone down with an acid tongue when it suited his purposes. He also had a lifelong problem with money. He was quick to borrow but slow to pay back. Despite his faults, however, Daniel Webster was now a young congressman on the rise to power.

The War of 1812

By the time Webster arrived in Washington, D.C., the War of 1812 was well under way. America was battling the British for freedom on the seas and to guarantee American independence.

Webster did not see eye-to-eye with Republican President James Madison and his party. The Federalists, and Webster in particular, blamed the war—which was hurting New England's trade—on the Republicans, and Webster did everything he could to sabotage the war effort. Henry Clay of Kentucky and John C. Calhoun from South Carolina both sided with President Madison. They tried to raise money for various war needs. Much debate took place in the House of Representatives between Calhoun and Webster.

Webster supported a strong, national government that had the final say in conflicts between the nation and the states. His opponents, who advocated states' rights, saw each state as superior and independent of the national government. Webster, hoping to embarrass the Madison administration, demanded reasons for the war. He claimed that France had tricked the president into starting a war with England.[4] Webster

Henry Clay (seen here) was one of Daniel Webster's chief adversaries during his early years in politics.

opposed every measure introduced in Congress to finance the war. He even opposed a bill encouraging army enlistment.

Webster seemed to view defeat on the battlefield as a problem for the party in power, not the country itself. He acted indifferently toward the war in the summer of 1813, saying, "The fact is, the Administration are, for the moment, confounded. They are hard pushed in our house—much harder in the Senate. They are in a sad pickle. Who cares?"[5]

Webster's first son, Daniel Fletcher, was born on July 23, 1813. For the time being, Webster wanted to put the war out of his mind and enjoy his growing family.

During the winter of 1814 to 1815, the country appeared to be near ruin. Still, Webster continued to oppose any measures to aid the war cause.

Then, a group of New England Federalists held a meeting in Hartford, Connecticut, from December 1814 to January 1815. They demanded constitutional reforms—apparently as the price for their part of the country staying in the Union. The meeting was known as the Hartford Convention. Webster had nothing to do with the meeting except to advise the New Hampshire governor against sending delegates. The convention mainly wished to register its protest against the war, but it was criticized for threatening the Union. Webster himself was later criticized for his minor role in the meeting.

The End of the War

Two events soon took place that saved the Union. First, the Treaty of Ghent, signed in Belgium on Christmas Eve, 1814, ended the War of 1812. John Quincy Adams, who led the American delegation in the peace process, remarked with some weariness, "I hope it will be the last treaty of peace between Great Britain and the United States."[6] Second, General Andrew Jackson was victorious against the invading British in the Battle of New Orleans on January 8, 1815. Although the war was technically over, news of the treaty had not yet arrived. Jackson's victory helped seal the peace agreement formally ending the war. These events made the Hartford Convention look foolish, and the Federalist party lost steady ground from then on.

Webster's Changing Views

Webster began to realize that, while merchants and ship owners lost much of their market and trading opportunities during the war, other segments of the economy, such as banking and manufacturing, had flourished. Men involved in shipping came to understand that their profits depended more on national markets than just local ones. Webster needed political seasoning to come to a more definite position. His next congressional term would help give him that experience.

5

GROWTH IN POWER

D aniel Webster was reelected to Congress on August 29, 1814. His first term had introduced him to the young United States government and how it functioned. Webster had discovered that he enjoyed politics. He was looking forward to beginning his new term.

Resolving Central Issues

Although Webster disapproved of many of the government's ideas, especially those set forth by Kentucky Congressman Henry Clay and South Carolina Representative John Calhoun, he could see benefits from some of them. The Federalist party had traditionally been nationalist. The Republican party was now slowly moving in that direction. The War of 1812 had changed Republican attitudes toward the national government. The Republicans now wanted to expand the home market and increase the country's military strength by developing roads and waterways. They also wanted to reestablish the national bank, which had ended in 1811. A strong national bank would stabilize currency and encourage business. They saw the value, too, in a high protective tariff. Webster's constituents could see the need for federal aid in helping with internal improvements, so Webster, too, supported federal aid.

Agreement on the bank issue proved more difficult. The Republican Madison administration hoped

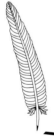

James Madison

James Madison served two terms as president, from 1809 to 1817. Born in Port Conway, Virginia, he entered politics in 1776. He played a major role in the Constitutional Convention of 1787, which created the United States Constitution. He also helped write *The Federalist Papers*, essays designed to win approval of the new Constitution. He was elected to the first national Congress and became a leader of the Democratic-Republican party.

Like Webster, Madison's political views changed over time. At first, he believed in a strict interpretation of the Constitution, with limited powers for the national government. By the end of his presidency, he had come to believe that the federal government should help fund such projects as roads and bridges.

for an institution that would be able to lend money to the government as needed. Webster, however, insisted on a conservative, independent bank. He believed the bank should be an institution that would "command the solid capital of the country," and one that would be attractive to "men of wealth and standing" to "embark their funds" in it.[1] New England was at an advantage here because it had more people, available funds, and sound banks than anywhere else.

New Horizons

By the spring of 1816, Webster was discouraged by the loss of Federalist power and by his own financial needs. He looked forward to finishing his congressional term. When he supported a bill to raise congressional salaries to $1,500 a year, he was amazed at the objections that were raised.[2]

Webster spent most of 1815 in Portsmouth. He was having trouble meeting his financial obligations and wanted to move his law practice to a more prosperous city, closer to Washington, D.C. He wrote to his brother Ezekiel, "Our New England prosperity and importance are passing away. If any great scenes are to be acted in this country within the next twenty years, New York is the place in which those scenes are to be viewed."[3]

When Webster's mother, Abigail, died on April 25, 1816, Webster's last family tie to New Hampshire was gone. To make matters worse, his house burned, destroying everything. Webster decided to move to Boston, Massachusetts.

After he and his family settled in Boston, Webster still had to finish his congressional term as a representative of New Hampshire. In October 1816, he and Grace left for Washington. They attended numerous dinners, balls, and social events. Webster even accepted a dinner invitation from President Madison.

The Websters' enjoyment of the capital was short-lived. They returned to Boston when their daughter Grace, who had been ill with what they thought was mumps before they left, grew sicker. Grace's death in January 1817 caused them great sorrow. Webster wrote to his brother Ezekiel: "Our dear little daughter followed yours. . . . Her disease, the consumption, had not apparently obtained its last stages. . . . when her countenance suddenly altered, & in five or six minutes she expired. Mrs. W. tho' in great affliction, is in tolerable health. . . ."[4]

After eleven days at home, Webster left his wife in the care of friends and tried to ease his own grief by throwing himself into his work. He remained in Washington until President

President James Madison led the opposing Democratic-Republican party during the first years Webster spent in Washington, D.C.

James Monroe's inauguration in March, then returned to Boston to resume his law practice. Nearly a year later, the Websters were cheered by the birth of another daughter, Julia, born on January 16, 1818.

The Kenniston Case

A short time after coming back to Boston, Webster's legal services were requested. The Kenniston brothers were toll keepers on the Exeter-Merrimack Bridge. Their case concerned Elijah P. Goodridge of Maine, who claimed that the brothers had assaulted, robbed, and shot him on the highway between Exeter, New Hampshire, and Newburyport, Massachusetts. At first, Webster declined to represent the brothers. He changed his mind when he learned that William Prescott, one of Boston's leading attorneys, was representing Goodridge. Webster felt it was a great challenge to go up against such an outstanding attorney. He arrived in Ipswich, Massachusetts, the night before the trial.

Word of Webster's appearance had spread, and the courtroom was packed. He had not been able to review the testimony or examine any witnesses ahead of time, but he listened carefully as Goodridge testified, recording each word in his memory. He planned to stake the case on his cross-examination. When his turn came to examine the witness, Webster applied his infamous dark scowl and growled at Goodridge. The witness became distraught and began to contradict himself. Webster then turned graciously to the jury and reminded them that their community had had a high reputation before Goodridge appeared. The jurors decided in favor of the Kenniston brothers, and Webster's reputation soared.

Over the next two years, Webster's fame grew with each case he tried. By the time he was forty, he was already becoming a legend.[5]

Boston Society

The Websters fit well into the upper crust of Boston society. The leaders of Boston were Federalists. Bostonians welcomed Webster because they trusted him to speak for their elite society. Webster represented well-to-do businessmen in the courts. They, in turn, invited him to buy stock in their corporations. He also received impressive fees for his legal services. Before long, Webster's yearly salary rose to twenty thousand dollars—at a time when common laborers earned only fifty cents a day. The move to Boston guaranteed that Daniel Webster would never lack opportunities. From now on, his fame—and his income—would rise accordingly.

6

ELOQUENCE
IN SPEECH

Webster's skill with words began to win him increasing fame. He was able to sway judges and juries, state constitution makers, visitors and colleagues in Congress, and huge audiences gathered for special occasions. William Plumer from the Republican party in New Hampshire said of Webster:

> His manner is forcible and authoritative. Nothing is left at loose ends in his statements of facts or in his reasonings; and the hearer passes from one position to another with the fullest conviction that the result must be correct, where the steps leading to it are so clear and obvious.[1]

The Dartmouth College Case

The Dartmouth College case began on September 19, 1817. It was the result of a quarrel between the Dartmouth trustees and the college's president, John Wheelock.

In 1816, New Hampshire's leading Republican officials wanted to make Dartmouth a state university. Because Wheelock opposed this, the trustees of the college fired him, and replaced him with Francis Brown. Wheelock asked New Hampshire's new Republican governor, William Plumer, for help. Plumer persuaded the state legislature to change the school's charter, making it a state university and renaming it Dartmouth University. By doing so, Wheelock could regain his presidency of the institution, since Francis Brown had been elected president of Dartmouth College, not Dartmouth University. Wheelock was appointed president of the university— so now there were two institutions of higher education fighting for the right to occupy the same campus. The struggle went to the courts.

When the case first came to trial before the New Hampshire Supreme Court, Daniel Webster joined Jeremiah Smith and Jeremiah Mason as part of the legal team for the college trustees. After Smith and Mason opened the argument, they said that the legislature had exceeded its authority and violated not only the state but the federal Constitution by altering the college charter, which had been granted to the school as a private institution. Webster and his side easily won this segment of the case. It moved next to the United States Supreme Court, presided over by Chief Justice John Marshall, a staunch Federalist.

Webster's speech to the Court lasted between three and five hours, beginning on the morning of March 10, 1818. He based his argument on the belief that the original charter was a contract that established a private corporation funded by financial gifts from private citizens. Webster said, too, that the Court had no power to allow the charter to be changed without threatening all similar institutions and their contracts.[2]

An artist's depiction of Daniel Webster (standing) making his famous argument in the Dartmouth College case.

Webster's closing speech, although not recorded, made a tremendous impact on the Court. The justices adjourned on March 14 without giving a decision. Webster did what he could during the summer and autumn recess to strengthen the college's position. He carefully revised his argument, then printed it and sent five copies to his friend on the Court, Justice Joseph Story, suggesting that he make copies available to any of the other justices.[3]

On February 2, 1819, Chief Justice John Marshall handed down the Court's famous decision, upholding the cause of the college trustees. Marshall said that the Dartmouth charter was a contract creating a "private eleemosynary institution."[4] The case hinged on the word *eleemosynary*, meaning related to charity. In other words, Dartmouth College was financed by gifts from individuals. Its charter could not be changed by the legislature without violating the Constitution.

The Dartmouth College case set an example for future cases. It also established Webster as the leading constitutional lawyer in the nation. Webster wrote to his brother Ezekiel before leaving the courtroom, "All is safe."[5] He considered the way "safe" for business investors who feared legislative interference in their pursuit of profits.

McCulloch v. Maryland

Webster argued two more important cases before the Supreme Court after the landmark Dartmouth College case. In *McCulloch* v. *Maryland*, Webster

Chief Justice John Marshall
Federalist Chief Justice John Marshall was born near Germantown, Virginia, in 1755. He studied law, and in the 1820s, became a supporter of the nationalist measures of George Washington and Alexander Hamilton. He served as secretary of state from 1800 to 1801, then was named Chief Justice of the Supreme Court by President John Adams in 1801. From his appointment until his death in 1835, he dominated the Supreme Court, helping to define its role and function and interpreting the Constitution in a large number of landmark cases.

argued that Congress had the power under the Constitution to create and maintain the Bank of the United States. He also argued that no individual state could legally tax the Bank because, by taxing, the states could possibly destroy the Bank. Chief Justice Marshall agreed with Webster's argument and handed down a decision based on the principle that the federal government was "limited in its powers" but "supreme within its sphere of action."[6] In other words, in cases of conflict, the national government was more powerful than state governments.

Family Joy

During 1820 and 1821, the Websters had two more children. Their son Edward was born on July 20, 1820. Another son, Charles, was born on December 31,

John Marshall, one of the most influential justices ever to sit on the Supreme Court, based many of his most enduring decisions on the arguments made by Daniel Webster.

The Plymouth Oration

Daniel Webster's Plymouth Oration, delivered on December 22, 1820, celebrated the Pilgrims' landing at Plymouth, Massachusetts:

> . . . *There is a local feeling connected with this occasion, too strong to be resisted; a sort of genius of the place, which inspires and awes us. We feel that we are on the spot where the first scene of our history was laid; where the hearths and altars of New England were first placed; where Christianity, and civilization, and letters made their first lodgement, in a vast extent of country, covered with a wilderness, and peopled by roving barbarians. We are here, at the season of the year at which the event took place. We cast our eyes abroad on the ocean, and we see where the little bark, with the interesting group upon its deck, made its slow progress to the shore.*[7]

1821. Daniel Webster loved his children dearly and delighted in playing with them whenever he was at home. While Webster spent time in Washington, however, his wife generally stayed in Boston with the children. Washington, still a very young city, lacked many necessities, including good schools for the children. Living their lives in two separate cities was hard on both Webster and his family. At times, Webster seemed to belong more to the nation than to his family.

7

ACCOMPLISHED STATESMAN

The 1820s turned out to be a time of triumph for Daniel Webster. He won court cases, gave eloquent orations, and received acclaim at every turn. Although his term as a congressman from New Hampshire ended in 1817, he never strayed far from the political spotlight.

At the time, Webster did not seem to be very interested in politics. However, he spent much of his time with politicians, especially those in Washington, D.C. He rejoiced in a new spirit of friendliness between the two political parties.

Constitutional Convention Delegate

As New England's most outstanding statesman, Webster was chosen to be a delegate to the Massachusetts

Constitutional Convention, which opened in November 1820. The most important issue the convention discussed was the forming of congressional districts. The state constitution of 1780 stated that representatives to the lower house were to be determined by the population in their districts. Senators, on the other hand, were divided into districts by amount of taxable property. The proposed move to change the constitution so that all legislators would be chosen according to population reflected the more democratic ideas of the time. Joseph Story, one of the Federalist delegates, objected to the proposal. He believed that giving too much power to poor people would threaten the protection of property.[1]

To the other delegates' surprise, Webster presented similar ideas. He claimed that political power without economic power invited lawlessness or a system of government in which one ruler has unlimited power. He was going against the popular idea that a district's population—not property—should determine both senators and representatives. In the end, despite much debate, Massachusetts kept its old methods of representation for both senators and representatives.

Spanish Claims Commission Cases

In December 1817, President James Monroe had ordered General Andrew Jackson to attack the Seminole Indians in Florida, which was then a Spanish possession. The tribe had continually crossed the border and attacked white settlements in Georgia. Jackson subdued the Indians, seized Florida, and sent the

Spanish governor fleeing to Cuba. But Jackson went too far. He killed two British subjects who were accused of aiding the Indians in their American raids. Nearly all of the president's Cabinet wanted to punish Jackson for his unauthorized action. But Secretary of State John Quincy Adams persuaded the president that it was in America's best interests to get Spain to sell Florida to the United States. Thus, Adams worked out a treaty with the Spanish.[2]

Under the Adams-Onís Treaty, the United States bought Florida for $5 million. This money was not paid to Spain, but to Americans who held claims

Adams-Onís Treaty

In return for agreement on boundary lines, the Spanish were ready to surrender Florida to the United States. The Spanish also gave up their claim to a huge area beyond the Rocky Mountains. The Spanish government was concerned that it would lose more territory in the Americas and in Mexico if it failed to establish definite boundaries with the United States. So, at the Spanish government's request, the Spanish minister, Luis de Onís, began in December 1817 to negotiate a treaty with John Quincy Adams, the United States secretary of state. In the Adams-Onís Treaty of 1819, Spain agreed to the sale of Florida and surrendered its claim to Oregon, while the United States gave up all claim to Texas. The United States also agreed to handle $5 million worth of monetary claims that Spain owed to American citizens.

Acquisition of Florida, 1819

▨ Occupied by United States 1810–1813

◩ Ceded to United States by Spain 1819

Through the settlement of the Adams-Onís Treaty, the United States bought Florida from Spain.

against the Spanish government. New England shippers, merchants, and insurance companies made claims under the treaty's terms. Webster defended many of them. His law practice flourished, and he made friends among the well-off families of merchants and shippers in cities along the East Coast. Webster was also becoming active in politics once again. In November 1822, Webster was elected as a congressman from Massachusetts to the House of Representatives.

The Steamboat Case

As Webster waited to take his congressional seat in December 1823, he was given a case involving Robert

Fulton's steam-propelled ship, the *Clermont*. Some years earlier, Fulton and his business partner, Robert Livingston, had acquired a monopoly from the New York legislature to operate steamboats in the waters surrounding New York State. Before long, this monopoly was contested by other steamboat companies. In the case of *Livingston* v. *Van Engen*, however, New York State's Supreme Court said that the monopoly would stand.

But in 1818, Thomas Gibbons bought a steamboat and began ferrying passengers from Manhattan to Elizabeth-Town Point, New Jersey. He was sued by Aaron Ogden, who had been operating a steamboat under a license from Fulton and Livingston. In 1824, Webster represented Gibbons before the United States Supreme Court.

Webster stated his main point in the case:

> That the power of Congress to regulate commerce, was complete and entire, and to a certain extent, necessarily exclusive; that the acts [of the New York legislature in creating this monopoly] in question were regulations of commerce, in a most important particular; and affecting it in those respects, in which it was under the exclusive authority of Congress.[3]

Webster argued that the state of New York had interfered with the exclusive right of the federal government to regulate commerce. Webster concluded by reminding the Court that he did not believe the Constitution had ever intended for the states to have the power to grant monopolies. The power to do so belonged to Congress alone. Chief Justice Marshall

David Claypoole Johnston drew this portrait of Daniel Webster, who was becoming one of America's most influential lawyers.

and the rest of the Court agreed with Webster. Gibbons was able to resume his steamboat business.

Webster was an important participant in five of the eight most outstanding constitutional cases decided by the Court from 1801 to 1824. The Court often seemed to hand down decisions based mainly on Webster's arguments. People began to call Webster the "Defender of the Constitution."

8

ULTIMATE POLITICIAN

A cclaim came to Webster from many directions. In August 1823, Dartmouth College granted Webster a Doctor of Laws degree in recognition of his "literary, scientific and professional eminence."[1] Webster's honorary degree seemed to influence voters in his November congressional election bid. He won by a majority vote of 2,638 to opponent Jesse Putnam's votes of 1,557. Webster took his seat in the House of Representatives on December 1, 1823.[2]

Financial Benefits

Although Webster enjoyed being in Congress, he still had a thriving law practice in Boston. When he served in Congress, his income went down. To remedy this situation, his supporters from the business community agreed to give or lend him money. Some businesses, like Boston Associates, also allowed him to buy shares in their companies. Thus, Webster looked to certain individuals and businesses to help support his increasingly lavish lifestyle.[3] Because Webster mixed with the upper classes of society, he and his wife often gave huge dinner parties. He also enjoyed having big houses, fine horses, and carriages, all of which cost considerable amounts of money.

Speech on Greek Independence

This time, Webster chose to bring his wife and children with him to Washington for his congressional term. Although he had not been in Congress for seven years, his regular Supreme Court appearances made it seem as though he had never left the capital. In addition, Webster's oratorical skills and legal ability had earned him an impressive group of admirers. This would be the first time in years, however, that members of Congress would witness his eloquence and skill. To remind his colleagues that he had political experience, Webster needed an opportunity to demonstrate his ability.

That opportunity came on January 19, 1824, when he spoke in Congress on the topic of Greek independence. When the Greeks began to fight for their independence from the Ottoman Empire in 1821, they looked to other nations for help in their struggle. Americans, in particular, could understand the Greeks' desire to be free. Webster's speech was masterful, but one question he asked was not well-received: "[I]s it not a duty imposed on us, to give our weight to the side of liberty and justice?"[4] Webster was suggesting only that America lend its moral support. But a number of Boston merchants traded with the Ottoman Empire. They did not want to lose business by having Congress support Greek independence. Webster's speech, though powerful, failed to earn him the credit he wished.

Judicial Reform Committee

Speaker of the House Henry Clay appointed Webster to chair the Judiciary Committee. In this position, Webster set out to reform and update the judicial system. One dilemma the courts faced was the addition of several new states to the Union: Mississippi, Indiana, Illinois, Alabama, Maine, and Missouri. At the time, federal judges traveled to the areas involved to hear cases. Supreme Court justices had to travel great distances to carry out their duties. Because they usually traveled by horse and carriage, much time was spent journeying between locations.

After many hours of discussing the issues, Webster and his committee failed to recommend necessary changes. Committee members offered several suggestions to remedy the problem, but could not agree on the changes. The committee's recommendations failed to please the House and were dismissed altogether. Webster was criticized for the failure. As Illinois Congressman John Wentworth noted, "he could give a fine speech on a particular subject, but not much else in the way of leadership to win passage of important legislation."[5]

Election of 1824

In the 1824 presidential election, no candidate received a majority of votes in the Electoral College. The final selection would have to be made by the House of Representatives. The choice was between John Quincy Adams and Andrew Jackson, both of whom were members of the Democratic-Republican party. Neither of the candidates especially suited Webster and his Federalist allies, though they leaned toward Jackson.

During Christmas vacation, Webster visited former President Thomas Jefferson at his Virginia home. Jefferson expressed alarm over the idea of Jackson's becoming president. Jefferson thought of Jackson as simply a military man with an explosive temper. Jackson was dangerous, Jefferson concluded.[6] When the House of Representatives voting began early in 1825, Adams narrowly defeated Jackson. Webster had voted for Adams.

Death Visits the Websters

While Webster was visiting Jefferson over Christmas in 1824, his little son Charles became very ill with pneumonia and died on December 19. Webster did not learn of his son's death until he returned to Washington. Although he did not show much emotion, he grieved deeply for his three-year-old son. To manage his sorrow, Webster immersed himself in the presidential decision of 1824–1825.

On June 17, 1825, the trustees of the Bunker Hill Association celebrated the fiftieth anniversary of the

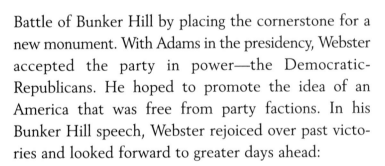

Bunker Hill
The Battle of Bunker Hill, which took place in 1775, the first full-blown battle in the American Revolution, was fought during the British siege of Boston when the American soldiers were pushed back from Bunker Hill in defeat. It was a memorable battle, especially to the people of Massachusetts. It was no surprise that they chose Webster to speak on the fiftieth anniversary of the battle.

Battle of Bunker Hill by placing the cornerstone for a new monument. With Adams in the presidency, Webster accepted the party in power—the Democratic-Republicans. He hoped to promote the idea of an America that was free from party factions. In his Bunker Hill speech, Webster rejoiced over past victories and looked forward to greater days ahead:

> . . . VENERABLE MEN! you have come down to us from a former generation. . . . You are now where you stood fifty years ago, this very hour, with your brothers and your neighbors, shoulder to shoulder, in the strife for your country. . . .
> Let us cultivate a true spirit of union and harmony. . . . And, by the blessing of God, may that country itself become a vast and splendid monument, not of oppression and terror, but of Wisdom, of Peace, and of Liberty, upon which the world may gaze with admiration forever![7]

The audience Webster addressed was estimated in the tens of thousands. When Webster came forward to

This portrait shows Daniel Webster as he looked around the time he delivered his famous address at Bunker Hill.

American politics changed greatly when Andrew Jackson, hailed as the first common man to be a successful politician, won the presidency.

From 1830 to 1832, Webster's life changed considerably. He bought and maintained a number of homes, including one in Washington and an estate at Marshfield, Massachusetts, in 1832. He continued to invest in and improve Marshfield over the years, no doubt thinking of it as a kind of legacy to the American people. He hoped one day he would be elected president of the United States.[1]

Staying in the Public Eye

Webster's desire to run for president increased after his debate with Robert Hayne in 1830. People around the country praised his speech and were becoming familiar with his name. He looked for opportunities to keep himself before the public eye.

On March 10, 1831, Webster attended a dinner given by National Republican leaders in his honor. At the time, National Republicans were forming a new political party to oppose the Democrats. It was called the Whig party. At the dinner, Webster was honored

The Whig Party

In nineteenth-century America, the Whig party formed to oppose the Jacksonian Democrats. Whigs favored high tariffs and a loose interpretation of the Constitution. The nineteenth-century Whig party was largely made up of people with wealth and culture, and those who opposed President Jackson.

for upholding the Union and the Constitution in the Hayne debate. The dinner was also being given to determine the public's interest in Webster as a presidential candidate. Several other possible candidates, including Henry Clay, John Calhoun, and Martin Van Buren, were also gearing up to run in the presidential race in 1832. Webster could do little but wait.

The Bank War

One of the causes Webster supported in Congress in May 1832 was a bill to recharter the Second Bank of the United States. Many people disliked the Bank, blaming it for earlier economic depressions. Those who supported it, like Webster, saw that it provided a stable currency, made national business transactions more convenient, and carried out operations for the United States Treasury free of charge.[2]

Thanks partly to Webster's efforts in the Senate on behalf of the Bank, the Bank Bill passed both houses of Congress. But President Jackson vetoed the bill on July 10, 1832. He claimed that the Bank Bill was

Changes—and the Polk Presidency

Democrat James K. Polk was elected president in 1844. Webster was reelected to the Senate in January 1845. As before, Webster's wealthy friends agreed to provide financing for him while he served in the Senate. This time, however, Webster suffered a misconduct charge for accepting money and gifts from Boston and New York businessmen while holding public office. Webster had accepted (and even asked for) money from these individuals so that he could represent them and their interests in Congress. Representative Robert C. Winthrop of Massachusetts defended Webster, saying, "He is here as no agent of private individuals. He holds his seat by the free and unsolicited suffrages [votes] of the Legislature of Massachusetts."[14] The Senate dismissed the charges against Webster on June 9, 1846.

Personal Losses

In addition to political troubles, Webster suffered two of his children's deaths in 1848. While serving in the army in Mexico, twenty-seven-year-old Edward contracted typhoid fever and died. At the time of Edward's death, Julia came down with tuberculosis. She died on April 28 at the age of thirty. A friend of Webster's, Peter Harvey, described Webster's grief:

> His whole expression was that of deepest grief. He seemed to be absorbed in a terrible struggle. . . . Mr. Webster threw himself upon the sofa in the parlor. . . . he burst into a paroxysm of grief, such as I do not think I ever before witnessed. He wept and wept, as if his heart would break.[15]

Edward Webster, Daniel's son, as he looked just a few years before his untimely death.

Political Crises

During this time, the United States was going through a new political crisis. In 1846–1847, Americans had fought and won a war against Mexico. By winning the war, the United States had gained new territories in the West, including what would become the states of California, New Mexico, and Arizona. People were eager to settle the new territories, especially after gold was found in California in 1848. However, the drive to settle the West caused serious issues to arise.

Northerners, who feared that the spread of slavery to new places would give Southerners too much political power, hoped to see the new territories become free states. Southerners, on the other hand, feared that the North was trying to gain enough political power to end slavery once and for all. To protect its way of life, the South hoped to expand slavery to new areas in the West. Through all this, politicians like Daniel Webster fought to preserve the Union.

In the election of 1848, Webster once more entertained the hope of becoming the Whig candidate for president. But the Whigs feared his past record of accepting money for his services would lose votes. In their search for a candidate, they turned to Zachary Taylor, a hero of the Mexican War. Taylor was a slave owner but had never said anything controversial about slavery. Although he thought the former general too inexperienced, Webster supported Taylor and the Whigs in the campaign. Taylor won the election and became president in 1849.

Soon, however, a crisis arose over the possibility of admitting California to the Union as a free state. This proposal angered Southerners, who hoped to spread slavery into the Western territories. Henry Clay offered a compromise: Admit California as a free state and open the territories of Utah and New Mexico to popular sovereignty—that is, let the settlers in these places vote to decide to become a slave state or free state. For the South, the compromise included a tough new Fugitive Slave Law. To please Northerners, Clay offered to abolish the slave trade—although not slavery itself—in the District of Columbia. The political arguments continued, with some Southern states even threatening secession. Webster felt powerless to reconcile the situation.

The Speech on the Compromise

Although he usually supported the interests of the antislavery North, this time, it seemed that compromise was essential if the Union were to be preserved. Daniel Webster stood before his Senate colleagues on March 7, 1850, and addressed them:

> I wish to speak today . . . as an American. . . . I speak today for the preservation of the Union. . . . I hear with distress and anguish the word "secession," . . . [I]nstead of speaking of the possibility or utility of secession . . . let us come out into the light of day. . . ; let us cherish those hopes which belong to us . . . let our comprehension be as broad as the country for which we act.[16]

Webster's speech focused on the Union. He offered no concrete solution for the nation's problems

Daniel Webster shocked Northern voters by favoring the Compromise of 1850. This is a page from his notes for the speech he delivered to Congress on March 7, 1850.

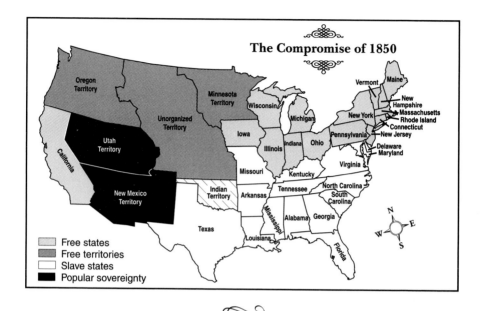

The Compromise of 1850

The Compromise of 1850 temporarily settled regional differences over slavery issues, but the questions would not go away permanently until after the Civil War.

beyond supporting the compromise, but stated that secession was not the answer. At his conclusion, the Senate chamber resounded with applause. People rushed to shake his hand. Webster's speech achieved its goal. The Compromise of 1850 was passed on September 20, 1850. However, Webster was bitterly attacked by many antislavery Northerners. They believed his willingness to compromise with the slave-holding South showed that he was not committed to the antislavery ideals of the North.

Secretary of State—Again

After Whig candidate Millard Fillmore was elected president in 1850, he appointed Webster to be secretary of state once again. Webster was delighted to have another opportunity to fill this influential office.

One of Webster's most significant accomplishments as Fillmore's secretary of state was the Clayton-Bulwer Treaty of April 19, 1850. The treaty arranged for Great Britain and the United States to encourage the building of a canal across Central America that neither country would seek to control. The treaty, it was hoped, would prevent future conflict between the United States and Great Britain as well as provide a more rapid way to travel from the Atlantic Ocean to the Pacific.

Such successes encouraged Webster. He now felt ready to pursue his lifelong ambition—to win the presidency of the United States.

10

FINAL DAYS OF HEARTACHE

Webster's speech in the Senate recommending the Compromise of 1850 spelled trouble for him. He thought this speech would serve to soften "political animosities" between Democrats and Whigs.[1] However, following the compromise, the Whig party in Massachusetts divided. Antislavery Whigs joined Free-Soil Democrats (who wanted to prevent slavery from spreading to new territories) to defeat the regular Whig candidates running for governor and senator. Webster saw a complete breakdown of the existing political parties. What he hoped to see, however, was another party. He said, "There must be a Union Party, & an opposing party under some name, I know not what, very likely the Party of Liberty."[2]

Presidential Ambitions

Taking their cue from Daniel Webster, several Northern businessmen and Southern planters sought to organize a Union movement. The businessmen wished Webster to head their presidential ticket in the upcoming election of 1852. But they wanted to interest the regular Whig party in their candidate, too. So they called a meeting to endorse Webster and to call Webster delegates to attend the Whig national convention in Baltimore. To their dismay, the first ballot gave Webster just twenty-nine votes—none of them from Southern delegates. President Fillmore received 133 votes and candidate Winfield Scott 131 votes. By the time the convention reached the fifty-third ballot, Winfield Scott had become the Whig candidate.

Webster was nominated as a presidential candidate by the Independent Whigs of Georgia and by the new American party. The situation, however, had become divisive. Some of Webster's friends urged him to distance himself from these new parties because they were taking votes away from the mainstream party, which could result in a presidential win by the Democrats. Webster replied bitterly,

> There is no equal number of gentlemen in the United States who possess more of my deep attachment and regard than the signers of your letter. But if I were to do what you suggest, it would gratify not only you and your friends but that great body of implacable enemies who have prevented me from being elected President of the United States.[3]

Despite the negative reaction of his fellow Whigs and the anger of many Northerners over Webster's support of the Compromise of 1850, Webster felt confident about his chances of winning the presidency.

Final Appearances

President Fillmore asked Webster to give a speech when the cornerstone for the new Capitol Building was laid on July 4, 1851. In his speech, Webster stressed the importance of maintaining the Union and its close relationship with liberty. He concluded with the same words to be engraved on the cornerstone:

> all here assembled . . . unite in sincere and fervent prayers that this deposit, and the walls and arches, the domes and towers, the columns and entablatures, now to be erected over it, may endure forever! GOD SAVE THE UNITED STATES OF AMERICA! Daniel Webster, Secretary of State of the United States.[4]

Some of those present thought Webster's performance was not up to his usual excellent standards and that he appeared unsteady on his feet. He was now sixty-nine years old and in declining health, suffering from bouts of rheumatism.

On February 23, 1852, Webster spoke to the New-York Historical Society. His speech discussed the importance of history. He made no mention of running for political office.

A month later, Webster argued his last important court case in the United States Circuit Court in Trenton, New Jersey. In it, he defended Charles Goodyear's patent for vulcanizing rubber.

This daguerreotype shows Washington, D.C., in the years before the Civil War. In the background, the unfinished Capitol, for which Daniel Webster helped lay the cornerstone, can be seen.

Carriage Accident

Shortly after arriving home at Marshfield on May 8, 1852, Webster and his private secretary were traveling in a horse-drawn buggy uphill toward a favorite fishing spot when the main carriage bolt broke. Seventy-year-old Webster was thrown to the ground. As he fell, he covered his head with his hands. His weight fell entirely on his arms and wrists. Both wrists were severely sprained. He also suffered a serious blow to his head, leaving a small flesh wound near his temple. The accident took a terrible toll on Webster. He suffered from dizziness and said and did strange things at times. He never fully recovered from the accident, and his health began to decline rapidly.

Boston Reception

Webster was still recovering from the accident when the political convention for president was held in June. He received scarcely any votes. He became bitter and depressed and began to drink heavily.

Looking for peace and solitude, Webster left Washington in early July for his farm in Franklin, New Hampshire. When he reached Boston, he received an invitation to a reception on July 9. The reception turned out to be an incredible showing of Boston's love and admiration for Webster. Almost the entire city came out to greet him. Hundreds of people came to the city by train, and posters with Webster's picture were everywhere. As he neared Boston, ringing bells signaled his entry into the city. With tears in his eyes, Webster gave a moving speech at Boston Common, expressing his appreciation and love for the city. The day did much to cheer Webster.[5]

Thoughts of Mortality

Because of his poor health, the summer months were difficult for Webster. More and more, his thoughts turned to death. He left Franklin for Marshfield on July 25, 1852. As he neared his estate, the road was thronged with people waving and cheering him with flowers and garlands. Upon his arrival at the house, one of his friends gave a welcoming speech. Webster returned the kindness with a brief speech, telling his friends how much they meant to him.

By September, Webster was in very poor health. His Boston physician, John Jeffries, and a local doctor named John Porter were both called to treat him. Nothing they tried, including applying leeches to his swollen stomach, seemed to work. Webster was urged to prepare his will.

In mid-October, Webster realized he was dying and cast himself "in the hands of God."[6] He also prepared an inscription for his tombstone, part of which read: "Lord, I believe; help Thou mine unbelief. . . . The Sermon on the Mount cannot be a merely human production. This belief enters into the very depth of conscience. The whole history of man proves it. Dan'l Webster."[7] In the inscription, Webster acknowledged God's help in making him the brilliant orator he was.

On October 18, Webster wrote a letter to President Fillmore, resigning as secretary of state. This was to be his last letter. On October 21, his condition worsened. At 8:45 P.M., Webster asked several people to witness his will. He left the bulk of his estate to his wife, Caroline, and to his son Fletcher. He asked each witness to approve his will and then said, "This is my last Will & Testament."[8]

For the next couple of days, Webster's friend Peter Harvey came to see him. Webster kissed him and said, "Kiss me. . . . I shall be dead tomorrow. . . . God bless you, faithful friend."[9] After midnight on Sunday, October 24, Webster suddenly revived and said, "I still live!"[10] Then he became still. The doctors came in and pronounced him dead.

Funeral for a Statesman

Church bells all over the nation tolled Webster's passing. Flags were lowered to half-mast. Webster had wished to be buried at Marshfield. On October 29, thousands of people, including Franklin Pierce (soon to be elected president), Governor Rufus Choate, the mayor of Boston, and many farmers, fishermen, and laborers thronged the roads leading to Marshfield.

Dressed in black trousers, a blue jacket with brass buttons, and a white vest, tie, and gloves, Webster's body lay in a coffin in the front yard. People filed by to gaze at the great statesman one last time. After a brief funeral service inside the house, the coffin was carried to a grave on the Marshfield estate.

The entire nation mourned Webster's passing. Preachers in their pulpits eulogized the great statesman, remembering the outstanding things he had done that made them proud to be Americans. Writer Ralph Waldo Emerson's words perhaps best summed up Daniel Webster's life: "The sea, the rocks, the woods, gave no sign that America and the world had lost the completest man. Nature had not in our days, or not since [French dictator] Napoleon, cut out such a masterpiece. . . . He was a statesman, and not the semblance of one."[11]

11

LEGACY

Often, only time provides enough distance to assess someone's life and achievement honestly. So it has been with Webster. While he lived, many praised his accomplishments as an orator, statesman, and lawyer. In each field, he excelled. He thrilled Americans with his reply to Hayne and his Bunker Hill address. Everything Webster believed found its way into his speeches. His overall theme, however, was always his concern for the Constitution and for the strength of the Union.

Although Webster's failures—his love of luxury, inability to handle money, and heavy drinking—were all too obvious while he lived, his outstanding qualities— his grace in diplomacy, his level-headedness, and his unusual reasoning ability—were sometimes taken for granted by his contemporaries. Arguing many landmark cases before the Supreme Court, he frequently broke new ground and helped set precedents that still have an impact on constitutional cases today.

As a statesman, too, Webster was invaluable. As secretary of state, he was ever vigilant to open new avenues for American commerce. Despite his vision for the United States, however, he retained his sense of stability and balance, moving cautiously in whatever situation he found himself. The many opportunities for establishing America's borders, reconciling opposing factions, and deciding the status of new states coming into the Union—whether slave or free—showed Webster's considerable strength.

Almost as a vindication of Webster's predictions, the Civil War broke out nine years after his death, when the Southern states chose to secede from the Union. At that time, Webster's ringing words— "Liberty *and* Union, now and forever, one and inseparable"—were spoken again, often by the Northern soldiers fighting to hold the Union together. Webster's cause had become their cause.

During the Civil War, United States President Abraham Lincoln sometimes used language similar to Webster's. In speeches such as the Gettysburg Address, he used themes that had been close to Daniel Webster's heart as he talked about the United States' being conceived in liberty for all people. Lincoln had the courage and wisdom to bring the Union back together. When the Union victory came in the Civil War after four long and bloody years, it was a victory

Artist John Pope painted this portrait of Daniel Webster, who remains one of the best-known statesmen in American history.

for liberty and Union. And Daniel Webster, though gone, had, in his own way, made an enduring contribution to the Union's success. Webster's great voice had been silenced by death, but even today, he can still be heard in the great speeches, debates, and court presentations he gave. Truly, Daniel Webster still lives.

CHRONOLOGY

1782—Born on January 18 in Salisbury, New Hampshire.

1797—Attends Dartmouth College.

1800—Delivers Independence Day address in Hanover, New Hampshire.

1805—Admitted to the Boston bar in March; Practices law in Boscawen, New Hampshire.

1807—Moves law practice to Portsmouth, New Hampshire.

1813—Begin to serve New Hampshire in the House of Representatives.

1816—Moves law practice to Boston.

1820—Delivers Plymouth Oration on December 22.

1822—Elected to serve Massachusetts in the House of Representatives.

1825—Delivers Bunker Hill oration on June 17.

1826—Elected to the Senate from Massachusetts.

1830—Debates Hayne in Senate.

1840—Campaigns for William Henry Harrison for president; Nominated as secretary of state; Harrison dies; John Tyler becomes president, and Webster remains as his secretary of state.

1850—Gives speech in favor of the Compromise of 1850 on March 7; Appointed secretary of state by Millard Fillmore.

1852—Dies on October 24 at Marshfield.

CHAPTER NOTES

Chapter 1. The Hayne Debate

1. *Webster's Speeches: Reply to Hayne* (Boston: Ginn and Company, The Athenaeum Press, 1897), p. 97.

2. Walker Lewis, ed., *Speak for Yourself, Daniel* (Boston: Houghton Mifflin, 1969), p. 178.

3. Robert V. Remini, *Daniel Webster: The Man and His Time* (New York: W. W. Norton & Company, 1997), p. 317.

4. Lewis, p. 194.

5. Richard N. Current, *Daniel Webster and the Rise of National Conservatism* (Boston: Little, Brown and Company, 1955), p. 61.

Chapter 2. Boyhood Days

1. Robert V. Remini, *Daniel Webster: The Man and His Time* (New York: W. W. Norton & Company, 1997), pp. 31–32.

2. Ibid., pp. 34–35.

3. Irving H. Bartlett, *Daniel Webster* (New York: W. W. Norton & Co., Inc., 1978), p. 17.

4. Ibid., pp. 18–19.

5. Ibid., p. 22.

6. Ibid., p. 24.

Chapter 3. Young Man on the Move

1. Charles M. Wiltse, ed., *The Papers of Daniel Webster, Correspondence, Vol. 1, 1798–1824* (Hanover: University Press of New England, 1974), p. 36.

2. David Crystal, ed., *Cambridge Encyclopedia*, 3rd ed. (Cambridge, England: University Press, 1997), p. 1118.

3. Irving H. Bartlett, *Daniel Webster* (New York: W. W. Norton & Co., Inc., 1978), p. 47.

4. Richard N. Current, *Daniel Webster and the Rise of National Conservatism* (Boston: Little, Brown and Company, 1955), p. 10.

5. Bartlett, p. 50.

Chapter 4. Up-and-Coming Congressman

1. Irving H. Bartlett, *Daniel Webster* (New York: W. W. Norton & Co., Inc., 1978), p. 53.

2. Ibid., p. 54.

3. Ibid., p. 55.

4. Richard N. Current, *Daniel Webster and the Rise of National Conservatism* (Boston: Little, Brown and Company, 1955), p. 15.

5. Ibid., p. 16.

6. John A. Garraty, *A Short History of the American Nation* (New York: Harper & Row Publishers, 1974), p. 118.

Chapter 5. Growth in Power

1. Richard N. Current, *Daniel Webster and the Rise of National Conservatism* (Boston: Little, Brown and Company, 1955), p. 20.

2. Irving H. Bartlett, *Daniel Webster* (New York: W. W. Norton & Co., Inc., 1978), p. 66.

3. Ibid.

4. Robert V. Remini, *Daniel Webster: The Man and His Time* (New York: W. W. Norton & Co., Inc., 1997), p. 149.

5. Irving H. Bartlett, *Daniel Webster* (New York: W. W. Norton & Co., Inc., 1978), p. 71.

Chapter 6. Eloquence in Speech

1. Richard N. Current, *Daniel Webster and the Rise of National Conservatism* (Boston: Little, Brown and Company, 1955), p. 27.

2. Irving H. Bartlett, *Daniel Webster* (New York: W. W. Norton & Co., Inc., 1978), p. 79.

3. Current, p. 32.

4. Bartlett, p. 80.

5. *The Orations on Bunker Hill Monument, The Character of Washington, and The Landing at Plymouth* (New York: American Book Company, 1894), pp. 88–101.

6. Geoffrey R. Stone, Louis M. Seidman, Cass R. Sunstein, and Mark V. Tushnet, *Constitutional Law*, 2nd ed. (Boston: Little, Brown and Company, 1991), p. 56.

7. Dartmouth College, "Plymouth Oration," *Daniel Webster: Dartmouth's Favorite Son*, n.d., <http://www.dartmouth.edu/~dwebster/speeches/plymouth-oration.html> (October 20, 2000).

Chapter 7. Accomplished Statesman

1. Irving H. Bartlett, *Daniel Webster* (New York: W. W. Norton & Co., Inc., 1978), pp. 81–82.

2. Robert V. Remini, *Daniel Webster: The Man and His Time* (New York: W. W. Norton & Company, 1997), p. 202.

3. Ibid., p. 208.

Chapter 8. Ultimate Politician

1. Robert V. Remini, *Daniel Webster: The Man and His Time* (New York: W. W. Norton & Company, 1997), p. 200.

2. Ibid.

3. Ibid., pp. 199–200.

4. Richard N. Current, *Daniel Webster and the Rise of National Conservatism* (Boston: Little, Brown and Company, 1955), p. 42.

5. Remini, p. 214.

6. Current, p. 44.

7. Dartmouth College, "The Bunker Hill Monument," *Daniel Webster: Dartmouth's Favorite Son*, n.d., <http://www.dartmouth.edu/~dwebster/speeches/bunker-hill.html> (October 20, 2000).

8. Irving H. Bartlett, *Daniel Webster* (New York: W. W. Norton & Co., Inc., 1978), pp. 91–92.

9. Ibid., p. 97.

10. Ibid., p. 110.

Chapter 9. Political Trials

1. Irving H. Bartlett, *Daniel Webster* (New York: W. W. Norton & Co., Inc., 1978), p. 123.

2. Ibid., pp. 128–129.

3. Ibid., p. 130.

4. Ibid.

5. Ibid., p. 136.

6. Richard N. Current, *Daniel Webster and the Rise of National Conservatism* (Boston: Little, Brown and Company, 1955), p. 66.

7. Ibid., p. 67.

8. Ibid., p. 69.

9. Robert V. Remini, *Daniel Webster: The Man and His Time* (New York: W. W. Norton & Company, 1997), p. 490.

10. Ibid., pp. 523–524.

11. Ibid., p. 530.

12. Ibid.

13. Ibid., p. 567.

14. Current, pp. 136–139.

15. Walker Lewis, ed., *Speak for Yourself, Daniel* (Boston: Houghton Mifflin, 1969), pp. 369–370.

16. Ibid., pp. 401–402, 408–409.

Chapter 10. Final Days of Heartache

1. Richard N. Current, *Daniel Webster and the Rise of National Conservatism* (Boston: Little, Brown and Company, 1955), p. 177.

2. Ibid.

3. Ibid., p. 179.

4. Robert V. Remini, *Daniel Webster: The Man and His Time* (New York: W. W. Norton and Company, 1997), p. 728.

5. Ibid., pp. 742–743.

6. Ibid., p. 756.
7. Ibid., p. 757.
8. Ibid., p. 759.
9. Ibid., p. 760.
10. Ibid.
11. Ibid., p. 762.

GLOSSARY

anarchy—An absence of government.

aristocratic—Upper-class or privileged.

compact—An agreement or contract between two or more parties.

declamation—A speech, often given as part of a school exercise.

despot—A person who holds power abusively or tyrannically.

eleemosynary—Relating to or supported by charity.

Federalist—A member of the political party that encouraged the increase of business and manufacturing, a strong central government, and friendly relations with Great Britain.

financier—Someone who handles money matters and investments.

nullification—The act of a state refusing to acknowledge or obey a law of the United States.

revolution—The overthrow of one government or ruler and the substitution of another.

rheumatism—Pain, stiffness, and swelling of the joints.

secede—Withdraw from an organization or political party.

tariff—Taxes (duties) imposed by a government on imported or exported goods.

venerable—Respected because of age or goodness.

FURTHER READING

Allen, Robert. *Daniel Webster: Defender of the Constitution.* Menton, Mich.: Mott Media, 1989.

Bartlett, Irving H. *Daniel Webster.* New York: W. W. Norton & Company, 1981.

Levinson, Isabel Simone. *Gibbons v. Ogden: Controlling Trade Between States.* Springfield, N.J.: Enslow Publishers, Inc., 1999.

Lodge, Henry Cabot. *Daniel Webster.* New York: Chelsea House Publishers, 1997.

Remini, Robert V. *Daniel Webster: The Man and His Time.* New York: W. W. Norton & Company, Inc., 1997.